NO NONSENSE INTERVIEWING

This book tells you:

★ What interviewers look for in job applicants

★ How to package yourself for success

★ The ten most commonly asked interview questions and their answers

★ Ten absolute interview don'ts

★ How you can get the job you really want

THE NO NONSENSE LIBRARY

NO NONSENSE CAREER GUIDES

How to Use Your Time Wisely
Managing People At Work/At Home

NO NONSENSE FINANCIAL GUIDES

How to Finance Your Child's College Education
How to Use Credit and Credit Cards, Revised Edition
Understanding Tax-Exempt Bonds, Revised Edition
Understanding Money Market Funds, Revised Edition
Understanding Mutual Funds, Revised Edition
Understanding IRA's, Revised Edition
Understanding Treasury Bills and Other U.S. Government Securities, Revised Edition
Understanding Common Stocks, Revised Edition
Understanding the Stock Market, Revised Edition
Understanding Stock Options and Futures Markets, Revised Edition
How to Choose a Discount Stockbroker, Revised Edition
How to Make Personal Financial Planning Work for You, Revised Edition
How to Plan and Invest for Your Retirement, Revised Edition
The New Tax Law and What It Means to You

NO NONSENSE REAL ESTATE GUIDES

Understanding Condominiums and Co-ops, Revised Edition
Understanding Buying and Selling a House, Revised Edition
Understanding Mortgages and Home Equity Loans, Revised Edition
Refinancing Your Mortgage, Revised Edition

NO NONSENSE LEGAL GUIDES

Understanding Estate Planning and Wills, Revised Edition
How to Choose a Lawyer

NO NONSENSE SUCCESS GUIDES

NO NONSENSE HEALTH GUIDES

NO NONSENSE COOKING GUIDES

NO NONSENSE PARENTING GUIDES

NO NONSENSE WINE GUIDES

NO NONSENSE CAREER GUIDE™

NO NONSENSE INTERVIEWING

How to Get the Job You Want

Phyllis C. Kaufman
& Arnold Corrigan

LONGMEADOW PRESS

No Nonsense Interviewing

Production services by William S. Konecky Associates, New York.

Published 1988 by Longmeadow Press, 201 High Ridge Road, Stamford, Connecticut 06904.

No Nonsense Career Guide is a trademark controlled by Longmeadow Press.

ISBN: 0-681-40141-9

Printed in the United States of America

0 9 8 7 6 5 4 3 2 1

To The Honorable Edmund B. Spaeth, Jr.,
a kind and wise judge who is
indeed "the true embodiment
of everything that's excellent."

ACKNOWLEDGMENT

The authors are indebted to Sanford L. Fox, Chairman, Fox-Morris Associates, Inc., for sharing his deep and extensive knowledge with us. We would also like to thank Herbert M. Adler, M.D., Clinical Professor, Departments of Family Medicine and Psychiatry, Thomas Jefferson University, and Julia Alexander, President, Legal Placements, Inc., for their generous contributions in the preparation of this book.

CONTENTS

INTRODUCTION TO INTERVIEWING

The job interview may be the most frightening part of your job search. But it can also be an exciting opportunity. It is your chance to convince one or more total strangers that you are the answer to their company's problems. Sound impossible? An awesome obstacle to gainful employment? Not at all. In fact, once you learn *how* to interview, each interview will become an interesting and stimulating challenge.

All you need is to understand a few basic interviewing techniques—and that's what this No Nonsense Career Guide is about. We will begin with a discussion of the three basic No Nonsense Interview Rules. Working on all aspects of these three will greatly increase your success rate. Then we will show you how to "package" yourself and how to handle the actual interview—proven techniques that will make you a powerful job candidate.

Learning how to interview requires work. There are no short cuts. But if you work hard and follow the advice given in this book, your results should improve spectacularly.

The three No Nonsense Interview Rules, which we will discuss in Part I, Be Prepared, are:

Learn How to Sell Yourself
Know the Company
Understand Your Interviewer

These rules should make it clear that interviewing is a serious business requiring clear thought on your part. You have to understand the company, the interviewer—and yourself.

One other bit of advice. Getting the *right* job requires time and patience. Employment specialists generally agree that you should expect to spend one month job hunting for every $10,000 of annual salary you expect to earn. If you are seeking a $50,000 job, expect your job search to take approximately five months. So be prepared—the right job is worth the wait.

PART I
BE PREPARED

PART I

1 · LEARN HOW TO SELL YOURSELF

An interview is a time of mutual evaluation, when you and the interviewer look each other over to see if a "match" is possible. An interview is never one-sided—it is an exchange of information. But most of all, an interview is a chance for you to sell yourself. It is an opportunity for you to communicate exactly what you can do and why you would be an outstanding employee. Don't expect an interviewer to unearth your wonderful hidden qualities. It's up to you to have enough respect for your own abilities to be willing to sell yourself—professionally but convincingly.

Understand Your Qualifications

The first step is to understand your qualifications. The Shakespearean saying "to thine own self be true" definitely

3

applies to job interviews. You must understand your strengths and weaknesses *before* the interview begins. Don't make the mistake of going into the interview without careful preparation. Get your act together before the curtain rises.

Know Your Strengths

You have already prepared your resume, listing your educational background, prior experience, and other relevant personal data. (For information on resume preparation, see the No Nonsense Resume Guide.) Now is the time to analyze your resume and, on a separate sheet of paper, list your strengths. What makes you special? What jobs are you especially suited for by your education, experience, talent, and special skills? Do you have other life experiences that give you additional qualifications for a certain position?

Think about items that do not appear on your resume. The interviewer can easily check your resume for a cold recitation of your education and experience. The interview is the time to talk about the things that make you especially interesting and valuable to this particular company.

For example, you may have discovered that you were a born leader when you were elected class president in college. Or your interest in caring for others may have begun when you started baby-sitting at age 12. Or you may have found that you worked easily with others and earned their respect while you were a Boy or Girl Scout working with your peers for merit badges. Or you may have discovered these same qualities in yourself more recently, in one of your previous jobs.

Some Examples

Lisa has an excellent resume showing her to be well educated and a creative writer. She is interested in a job in publishing and is willing to begin as a copy editor in order to work her way up to being a full-fledged editor.

While her resume is strong in academic skills, Lisa wants to emphasize her broad knowledge of literature and her understanding of the publishing business. She has never worked in publishing before, but her Uncle Marvin once owned a small publishing house that specialized in books of a technical nature. Obviously, there is no place for Uncle Marvin on Lisa's resume. But Lisa makes a mental note to mention the experiences she had of visiting her uncle's office, touring his printing plant, and discussing the publishing business with him when she was younger. She also vividly recalls going to bookstores with her uncle while he explained book merchandising to her.

These experiences, while not fitting into a resume, are excellent conversational items for Lisa to bring up during interviews with publishers. They help to make Lisa unique and to give her a certain edge over other candidates for the position. At the very least, discussion of these experiences should move the conversation along in directions that will be favorable for Lisa.

Robert is another good example of how to use an often overlooked life experience as an interview plus. Robert was recently graduated from law school and is interested in labor law representing unions. He has always been interested in labor law because his grandfather was one of the founders of the bricklayers union in Brooklyn, and his father and four uncles are all active union members. Union organization, activities, and problems always fascinated Robert and were an ever-present part of his life. His family history in the labor movement does not appear on his resume, but it is something that Robert can use in interviews to distinguish himself from other candidates and to show his dedication to, and understanding of, his chosen profession.

Know Your Weaknesses

It may be even more important to know your weaknesses and points of vulnerability than to understand your strengths. Just as a chain is only as strong as its weakest link, the sum of your qualifications may be only as strong as your greatest weakness.

Check your resume and make a list of points of vulnerability. Analyze your weaknesses (and seeming weaknesses) so that you understand and can explain them. For example, have you been unemployed for a period of time? When? Why? Perhaps there is a favorable explanation, such as taking time off to continue your education. Have you ever been fired from a job? Why? Is there any way in which you can explain the firing as a positive experience?

We strongly suggest that you have the courage to bring up obvious weaknesses yourself rather than waiting for the interviewer to catch them. When you voluntarily bring up and explain a weak point, you prevent the interviewer from suspecting that you have something to hide.

Here are a few suggestions as to how you might cast negatives in a positive light. If you were once fired from a job because you didn't relate well to your boss and peers, you might explain the firing in this way:

> I used to be very intense, eager to accomplish a lot, and unable to work with people who didn't work at my fast pace. I think that I have matured, and while I am still very eager to accomplish and to reach my goals, I have become easier to work with and more understanding of the needs of others. I definitely now consider myself a team player.

You could handle a period of unemployment in this way:

> Several months ago I realized that I wasn't happy with my job because I didn't find it as stimulating as I had expected. You see, I consider myself a very creative person, and while this job in advertising sounded creative, the reality was that I spent the great majority of my time doing endless paperwork.
>
> While I don't mind paperwork and I know that as a good manager I will have paperwork to do, I felt that I was being smothered in masses of paper. I left the job, under very amiable circumstances, in order to

reconsider the direction of my life. This thoughtful time has been a big help to me, and I think that I now understand exactly what type of job I want and can do best.

Be Special

While memorability is your goal, you must never abandon good taste. You want to be unique, but not outlandish. So be tempered in your behavior and act so that you will be remembered in a positive way.

2 · KNOW THE COMPANY

Prior to any interview, you must find the answers to two essential questions. What can you do for this company? And why do you want to work there?

The only way you can answer these questions intelligently is by taking the time to study the company and its goals. Such research may be time consuming, but it is absolutely necessary. As one professional interviewer said, "Why should I think that you will be a conscientious and well-prepared employee if you haven't taken the time to prepare for the interview?"

Why Research Is Important

The fact that you have taken the time to research a company and learn about it is a compliment to the company and the interviewer, and will increase your chances of success. Also, the research you have done into the company shows the quality of initiative on your part. Finally, after all this research, the fact that you are now applying for the job shows that you like what you have discovered. This is a compliment both to the company and to the interviewer who already has the good sense to work there.

Sources of Research

The library is the best place to begin your research. Magazine articles about the company will be listed in the *Reader's Guide to Periodical Literature*. Some of the major newspapers publish indexes (in some cases computerized) so that you can quickly determine if the company has been in the news. Check the newspapers for information or any news stories about the company, its personnel, and the industry in which it operates.

Many libraries, and especially business-oriented libraries, will also have annual reports and prospectuses of individual companies. If the company is publicly owned and your library does not receive its reports, call the company, ask for the office of the secretary or treasurer of the company, and ask them to send you an annual report, a recent prospectus, if available, and any marketing brochures or other information that will tell you about the company. The company will usually be glad to send these upon request to interested members of the public.

If the company is publicly owned, there are many other sources of financial information available, the best known of which are *Moody's Manuals* and *Standard and Poor's Corporation Records*. These are available at many local libraries and at virtually all college libraries.

If the company is not publicly owned, information may be more difficult to obtain, particularly financial information. Start, again, with magazines and newspapers. Ask your librarian for any industry directories or general corporation directories that might be helpful. If you have access to Dun and Bradstreet credit reports, by all means obtain a report on the company. Your bank may possibly be helpful in obtaining this research material.

Contact People

Whenever possible, talk to people who have worked for the company or in its industry, or who are in any way familiar with it. Talk to friends or relatives who are in the same business. Learn what you can about the business, even if it doesn't relate specifically to this individual company.

What to Look For

Use the company reports and other material to learn about the company's operations, its products or services, and its organization and management structure. Study the sales and profits figures, if available. Learn where the company has branches, subsidiaries, and plants. Find out where and to whom it sells.

The company's history is most important. How has it grown? How does it compare to its competitors? What is the outlook for the industry? What is its future? How does recent technology affect it? Are there advances that are still in the research stage that will have great impact on the industry in the future?

Look into the product lines and their offshoots. Where is the company going and how can you help take it there? Will there still be a need for its products in 10 or 20 years? How should the company and/or its products change or expand in preparation for the 21st century?

Obviously, you are not likely to be able to answer all the above questions—nor would we expect you to, unless you have had long experience in the industry and are applying for a job at the level of vice president or higher. But learn all you can. The more you can learn about the company, the better prepared you will be.

Think!

Needless to say, you should not approach your research as a mission to accumulate statistics. That's not the point. The purpose of your research is to give you the ammunition to think about the company, its future, and how you can fit in. The interviewee who understands the workings of the company and its industry stands a much greater chance of success than a candidate who didn't care enough to do the necessary homework.

As you digest and analyze the facts you have researched, think how you can use them to your advantage in the interview. Certain facts about the company may help you stress your own abilities and qualifications. For example, "Company X is a multinational corporation, and with my fluency in Spanish, I believe that. . . ." Information about the company may also help you toward more general comments. If sales and market share are on the rise, you might say that this is where you want to be—at the forefront of the industry. If they are on the way down, you might suggest that the company needs someone with your energy, good attitude, and excellent ideas to help reverse the trend.

Try to carve a niche for yourself in the future of the company. Remember, in order to assure success, you must be special and memorable. Research is your first key.

3 · UNDERSTAND YOUR INTERVIEWER

Your next big unknown is the person who will be facing you in the interview. Of course, interviews may be conducted by more than one person (see Chapter 8), but even in those multiple-interviewer situations, the technique for understanding your interviewer is the same. In the latter case, there are simply more of them for you to understand.

The Interviewer's Job Is on the Line

If the interviewer makes a bad decision and hires the wrong person, it will reflect badly on him/her. So your first job is to make the interviewer comfortable with the conclusion that you are absolutely the best person for the job. You know that you have some faults, but they can be turned to your advantage or at least neutralized. Meanwhile, your research into the company and industry, and your understanding of the stress that interviewing puts on the interviewer, will make you an outstanding candidate.

The Interviewer Wants to Like You

The interviewer probably wants to fill this job as quickly as possible. If the organization needs a new person, it probably needs that person *now*. You can make this process easier for both of you by presenting yourself in a manner that makes the interviewer understand that you are the right choice.

Make Him/Her Comfortable

Try to make the interviewer comfortable with you. Professionals call this "falling in step with the interviewer," that is, making the interviewer feel that there is something about you that he/she feels comfortable with. In fact, psycholo-

12

gists often suggest trying to make the interviewer see himself/herself in you.

So, try to find something in common with the interviewer whenever possible. Try to interject some personal bit of information that will put him/her at ease. For example, if there is a very beautiful painting or other art work on the wall, you might comment about it. Or, if the person's desk is of exceptionally interesting wood, you might say, "You rarely see desks made of that fine rosewood these days. Was the desk made for you?" Of course, this could backfire if all the desks were made like this and the rosewood you so admired was only a thin veneer over a steel frame. So be careful to limit your compliments or comments to those things on which you are knowledgeable.

PART II
PACKAGING YOURSELF FOR SUCCESS

PART II

4 · FIRST IMPRESSIONS

First impressions are usually lasting. That is why this chapter is devoted to making your first impression positive, appealing and winning.

There are many words that can be used to describe the first impression you want to convey. These include polite, confident, sincere, courteous, tactful, actively interested, and interesting. While enthusiasm about yourself and the job under discussion is very appealing, you must take care not to be overly bubbly. You should never discuss irrelevant personal matters. You should never complain about your former job or about anything else. And you should never speak ill of anyone, especially not a former employer.

Smile

A smile combined with a positive attitude is contagious and wins jobs.

Be Polite

No matter how excellent your credentials are and how well educated you are, it is worth remembering that the person who is interviewing you has one thing you probably don't have—a job. Even if you have a Ph.D from Harvard and the interviewer never went to college, he/she is in the driver's seat as far as your getting a job is concerned, so remember the first rule—be polite.

A polite and respectful attitude toward everyone, from the elevator operator and receptionist to the interviewer, creates a favorable impression. How you will work with others is indicated by how you treat people. So always try to convey a polite first impression.

Never Lose Your Cool

Never lose control. No matter how outrageously the interviewer may behave, you must never be impolite or arrogant. We know of one interviewer who regularly keeps interviewees waiting several hours, without giving an excuse, just to test their patience and how much they actually want the job. Then there is the "silent treatment," which we'll discuss in Chapter 8. No matter what happens, never be arrogant and don't lose your self-control.

Nervousness

Some nervousness is natural. However, the more responsible the position, the less nervousness and the more confidence you should display.

Preparation is the best way to reduce nervousness. It won't stop it altogether, but doing your homework really helps. And always remember: If you don't get this job, you aren't any worse off than you were before, and you will have learned something about how to handle future interviews.

Control Your Hands

Don't let your hands convey tension. Your hands can give away more information than you intend. For example, never grab the arms of the chair and clutch them tightly. This is too tense for the interviewer to be comfortable with you. Don't knot your fingers together in a tight ball. Such action also shows tension. Don't fold your arms about you defensively. This indicates you may have something to hide. Don't stroke your hands together, twiddle your thumbs, or play with your clothing or hair. Your hands can betray your confidence. Practice keeping them relaxed looking and still.

Hands That Shake

Here's a trick to stop your hands from shaking. Before you go into the interview room, make a tight fist with each hand. Squeeze as hard as you can without injuring yourself. Feel all the tension from your arms go into your hands. Hold the squeeze. Then relax your hands and shake them out—not too hard, but vigorously enough to release all that built-up tension. Then, when you go into the interview room, your hands should be relaxed (or exhausted). In either case, they shouldn't shake.

Clammy Hands

That cold, clammy feeling you get when you are nervous or waiting for something to happen is as unpleasant for the person who has to shake your hand as it is for you. A clammy handshake may dampen your chances of getting the job.

We suggest arriving at your appointment early enough so that you can get to the rest room and wash your hands before the interview. Dry them thoroughly. Then, just before you enter the interview room, wipe them off on a tissue to make sure that they aren't clammy.

One friend of ours suffers from clammy hands and has discovered a solution we'd like to share with you. She puts a bit of antiperspirant on her hands before leaving her home, and her hands are clammy no more!

The Handshake

A handshake is the only physical contact you will have with your interviewer. It must convey a positive impression. Your handshake should be firm, but not painful. A limp handshake is not appealing, but be careful not to be so firm as to cause pain. Try practicing on a friend. Grip the other person's hand firmly, but not too tightly, shake only briefly, and then let go.

It is quite appropriate to shake hands at the beginning and at the end of your interview. However, if you did not shake hands at the beginning, definitely offer your hand to the interviewer at the end. The feeling of firm acceptance and cordiality is exactly the final impression you want to convey.

While etiquette traditionally cautions that a gentleman never extend his hand to a lady, this rule has been abandoned in the workplace. It is sometimes best for the interviewee to wait until the interviewer extends his/her hand. However, if that seems awkward, there is nothing wrong with the interviewee taking the initiative.

Your Voice

The one sure clue to nerves is your voice—it will rise in pitch when you are nervous. A calm, confident, controlled person is usually in command of a well-modulated, relaxed voice.

Modulated Voice, High Power

Relaxation is the key to keeping your voice well modulated. Here are a few exercises you can do just before your interview to make sure that your voice doesn't betray your nervousness:

Put your lips together and begin to hum the letter *M*. As you hum, try to bring your voice forward in your mouth so that your lips begin to vibrate. Continue doing this until you feel secure that your voice is placed forward in your mouth.

Second, open your mouth about two fingers wide and, while keeping your mouth open, *whisper* the letter *L*, using only your tongue for articulation, not your lips. Then try whispering *N*. Once you begin speaking, you will find that this exercise has returned your voice to its normal pitch.

Do a Vocal Check

During your interview, try to keep your voice well modulated, and check on yourself periodically. If you find that you are speaking in a higher than normal register, consciously lower the pitch of your voice, not its volume.

How Loud?

Moderation is the key. Some people tend to speak softly when they are nervous. If the room is large, or if you are being interviewed by more than one person, it is essential that you keep your voice at a level where you can easily be heard. This doesn't mean that you should shout, but projecting your voice is necessary.

Body Language

Body language often "speaks" louder about you than what you say. A person who cringes defensively in the chair with hands folded protectively around his/her torso is displaying the obvious body language of a shy and reticent individual. If this person is applying for a sales or managerial job, the body language will not match the job description, no matter how articulate the person may be.

You want to maintain a body language that conveys a confident and positive attitude. If you are applying for a supervisory position, you want to convey authority without being authoritarian. You should always try to convey through your body language a demeanor that would fit a job one level above the one for which you are applying.

Think About Posture

Good posture makes a good impression. Erect carriage is the mark of confidence; slouching, of sloppiness. However, don't confuse good posture with tension, and always convey confidence, not discomfort. While ramrod-straight military bearing is essential if you are in uniform, in civilian life such a stance can be perceived as tense, formidable and overbearing.

Legs

This section is especially important for women, although men should also be aware of potential problems, especially with so many female executives now interviewing male applicants.

Keep your knees together—always. You may sit with both feet firmly on the floor (most comfortable for men), or cross them at the ankle, or one on top of the other. The only rule is always to keep your knees together.

Eyes

Try to look at your interviewer and direct your answers directly to him/her. Shifty-eyed candidates rarely get job offers. If you are thinking and let your eyes wander around the room, make sure that you return your gaze directly toward the interviewer when you are answering his/her questions. And always look at the interviewer when he/she is addressing you, even if the interviewer gazes in another direction.

If more than one person is interviewing you, always look directly at the person who is speaking to you. Begin your answers to any question by directing your gaze at the questioner, then try to include the other people in the room in your gaze as you respond.

Hands and Arms

What to do with your hands and arms is always a problem. If you generally gesture with your hands when you talk, don't try to stop that during an interview. You will only feel uncomfortable, and your discomfort will come through. However, if you aren't used to talking with your hands, this is not the time to start. Instead, try to keep your hands relaxed and placed in your lap or on the arms of the chair.

The Telephone

It is more than likely that your first personal contact with the interviewer will be on the telephone, setting up the interview. Make sure that your voice is clear and not squeaky, flat or expressionless. Before an important telephone conversation, it often helps to warm up your voice by talking out loud or doing the vocal exercises mentioned earlier in the chapter.

If you don't know how you sound on the telephone, ask a friend to help you practice setting up an interview on the telephone. Or practice with a tape recorder, so that you understand how your voice sounds.

If you tend to get flustered easily, try jotting down some notes about what you want to say, but be careful that your conversation doesn't sound memorized.

Screening by Phone

It is not unusual for an employer to use the phone to screen applicants. This is especially true if using the telephone is an important part of the job description.

Be prepared before you pick up the phone. Remember to be brief and to the point. Have your resume in front of you so that you can refer to it if questions are asked about your qualifications.

Remembering Names

Nothing creates a poorer first impression than forgetting the interviewer's name, or mispronouncing it. Here is a technique you can use to help you remember names. You will find it especially helpful when there are more interviewers than one.

As you are introduced to each person in turn, shake their hand and repeat their name. The lead interviewer will probably introduce each person to you. Or sometimes each person will introduce him/herself. After each introduction, you can say, "Nice to meet you, Mr. Wolfson," or, "It's a pleasure to meet you, Ms. Langdon." By repeating the person's name, you reinforce it in your mind, which will help you to identify each person by name later.

Some people recommend quickly jotting down each name when you sit down, but we find this awkward in most circumstances. We think that concentrating hard and repeating the names upon introduction is the best procedure.

5 · WHAT TO WEAR

How you dress for an interview, or how you "wrap" your package, is a topic that easily deserves its own chapter. Too many jobs have been lost by otherwise qualified candidates because they failed to heed a few simple rules.

First, always dress for an interview as if you were applying for a position one step higher on the corporate ladder. That is, if you are applying for an assistant manager position, dress as if you were applying to become manager—and so on.

Second, dress so that you fit in with the environment and style of the company. Be conservative, never strange or outlandish. Your goal is to look like someone the interviewer will want to work with and get to know. When you are selecting what to wear, always keep carefully in mind the impression you are trying to make.

Basics

Too much of anything is not appropriate. The best rule is *dress conservatively.* Don't wear too much jewelry, cologne, perfume, or makeup, and by all means use mouthwash and deodorant.

Always be neat and clean. Freshly washed, cut, and groomed hair, clean hands and fingernails, shined shoes, freshly creased trousers, a clean and well-ironed shirt, are all musts. And since eye contact is important (see Chapter 4), don't wear sunglasses. Of course, you should never wear jeans.

Why Fuss About What to Wear?

Many people, especially those looking for their first job, think that they should be hired on merit and not because of the way they look or dress. We understand that feeling, but we assure you that even if you have an honors MBA from Harvard, you will not get the job if you appear at a corporate interview in jeans. In fact, you may not be allowed in the office. Your merits will never be displayed because your appearance shows that you don't know how to fit into the corporate environment. You may be creative and brilliant, but without the common sense to dress appropriately, no company will want you.

Keep a Record

We suggest that you keep a written record of what you wear to each interview on your interview recap sheet. (See Appendix C.) Note all the details of your wardrobe, right down to the shoes and jewelry. Then, if you are asked back to the office for a second interview, you will have a record of what you previously wore so that you won't duplicate it. However, if your first interview is with the personnel department and you don't expect to see that interviewer again, you can repeat the same outfit at your next interview.

Coat and Hat

Try to leave your coat, hat, umbrella, boots, and other outerwear with the receptionist before entering the interview room. If there is no place to do this, remove your coat prior to entering the room and carry it, so that you don't have to fumble while removing it. Try to be as unencumbered as possible when entering the interview room.

Dressing for an Interview—Men

As men and women have different problems to consider in dressing for an interview, we'll discuss each separately, beginning with men.

Suits

A man should always wear a conservative three-piece or two-piece suit to an interview. A sports jacket is not appropriate.

The best suit colors are navy blue and dark gray. A darker suit gives the perception of greater authority, but don't wear black—it's too funereal. A subtle pinstripe is an excellent choice, with solid navy or gray good alternatives.

The suit should be wool. Polyester or a polyester blend doesn't have the "feel" of success. Be careful of wool and silk blends, which, while expensive, can look shiny in some lights. Never wear a linen or linen blend because it wrinkles.

One other suit tip. No matter how warm it is, never take your suit jacket off—unless the interviewer suggests it.

Shirt

Your shirt must be wrinkle-free and crisply ironed.

A solid white shirt is always best. Solid light blue is also acceptable. We do not recommend pink, yellow, green, or any blue other than the palest. Of course, you must match your shirt to your suit, and we suggest that you get professional advice at the store where you purchase your suit. Tell your salesperson that you are going to use the suit for an interview, and have him/her help you select an appropriate shirt and tie.

Tie

You must always wear a tie. Studies show that bow ties command less respect than conventional ties. Silk is the preferred material for ties, although some high-grade polyesters that look like silk are acceptable.

Never let your tie be lighter than your shirt and suit unless you want to look like the archetypical gangster.

Solid ties are safe, but tend to be uninteresting. The best ties are those with a small regularly repeating pattern such as a subtle polka dot, small foulard, or regimental stripe (known as a "rep" tie). The pattern or stripe should coordinate with your shirt and suit and be pleasing to look at. It should not call attention to itself or make a statement. Do not wear a tie with a pattern that spells anything or is the symbol of any fraternal, religious, or political organization.

Belt and Suspenders

Keep belts plain and coordinated with the suit. Never make a statement with your belt. Suspenders may be worn as long as they are conservative.

Jewelry

Less is definitely better. Big, flashy rings should be left home on interview day. A school ring, initial ring, or wedding band is appropriate. Cufflinks, if worn, should be conservative and simple and should not attract attention. Visible neck chains, pins, buttons, or other religious or fraternal ornaments should be omitted.

Shoes and Socks

Conservative black or dark brown shoes and dark socks are best. Never wear white socks. Your socks must coordinate with your shoes, and your shoes with your suit. Ask your suit salesperson to suggest a shoe color if you are in doubt, or take the suit with you to the shoestore. Remain conservative right down to your toes.

Make sure that your shoes are freshly polished for each interview and that your socks don't slip down. Small grooming touches of this sort are a mark of your respect for the interviewer and the company.

Carry a Briefcase

You ought to take extra copies of your resume with you, and they should never be hand carried. (See Chapter 7.) The best and most professional carrier is a leather briefcase. If the briefcase has initials on it, make sure that they are yours.

Carry all your important items in the briefcase. Don't have bulges in your suit pockets—this gives an unkempt appearance.

Pens and Pencils

It is wise to carry a pen and pencil in your breast pocket, in case you must take notes or fill in an application. A simple gold-toned or silver-toned pen and pencil are acceptable. A regular pencil is out; you must have a mechanical one. Make sure that your pen doesn't stain your suit, and never put pens or pencils in your shirt pocket.

What to Wear—Women

Conservative and *expensive* are the two hallmarks for successful female interview dressing.

A Suit

A suit is the safest choice, no matter what type of job you seek. Select a simple, well-fitting suit with a modest skirt. If the suit is too tight, the interviewer, especially if it is a man, may get the wrong impression. The same approach holds true for skirt length. Never wear a miniskirt, no matter how stylish they are. You can wear a skirt that is just above the knee if the skirt is not too tight and if you can sit and cross your legs comfortably and without embarrassment.

Select the suit color carefully. Try for a color that is flattering but not flashy or too vivid.

The best suit colors are navy, black, beige, medium blue, gray, and deep green. Wild or loud patterns are distracting and never a good choice, but the suit doesn't have to be solid. A tweed or conservative stripe is fine, as is a muted plaid.

Wool is the best fabric, with wool crepe a good all-season compromise. A silk blend is fine, as long as it doesn't appear shiny. Remember that linen wrinkles and that the wrinkled look is never proper for interviews. Polyester and polyester blends do not convey the stylishness of wool or silk.

Blouse or Sweater

A blouse is always preferable to a sweater. A sweater can easily be misinterpreted as either too sexy or too casual. A conservative blouse with a modest but feminine neckline is most suitable. A jewel neck, stock tie, simple collar, or modest scoop or V-neck are all good choices. Try to avoid ruffles and fussiness. Make sure that the blouse looks good with your suit and that the collar doesn't require constant adjusting. Check to see if you need a belt to give a completed look.

Skirts and Tops

We do not recommend wearing a separate skirt and a top, whether a blouse or a sweater, to an interview. A skirt and top are simply too casual for professional acceptance, and since you are striving to dress one level above the job for which you are applying, this outfit isn't appropriate.

Dresses

We like dresses, and wearing a dress to an interview is an option, although traditionally considered an adventurous one. There are many conservative, flattering dresses available today. Silk or wool are the preferred materials, but some high-grade polyester looks so much like silk that it's very difficult to tell the difference.

Again, we want to emphasize that wearing a dress is not the norm for interviews. A suit is safer. But if you really want to wear a dress, here's what to look for.

The dress should be conservative in color and style. Let it be not too tight or too figure revealing. Keep the color simple and the pattern, if any, modest and not fussy. Try to avoid flashy colors. The fact that you are wearing a dress is enough of a deviation from the norm; don't compound it by wearing chartreuse or a pink and black stripe.

The neckline should be conversative and not too low cut. Don't buy a dress or blouse where you have to pin the neckline closed; this never quite works, and it gives a sloppy appearance.

Skirts

Always try sitting in the suit or dress skirt before you buy it, or at least before you wear it to the interview. Is it comfortable? Does the skirt ride up embarrassingly? Can you cross your legs and still protect your modesty? Does the skirt wrinkle after you sit?

Then try looking at yourself with back lighting. Do you need to wear a slip?

Trousers and Pantsuits

Trousers and pantsuits are not acceptable for interviews unless you are applying for a job in some rough location, say in forestry or geology, where you might encounter difficult terrain as part of the job and even during your interview.

Hose and Shoes

Always wear sheer hose. No matter how hot it is, no matter how uncomfortable they may be, they are a must. Match your hose to your shoes and your suit or dress. If you want to be ultraconservative, wear natural-colored nylons.

One important tip is always to carry a spare pair of hose in your briefcase, in case you get a run. When you arrive at the interview, you can always slip into the ladies room and change your hose, if necessary. This is especially important with darker shades, where a run is more obvious.

Shoes are very important, as they complete your outfit. A little extra investment in a better-quality shoe is never a mistake. They should be conservative and sensible. Never wear shoes in which you have difficulty walking. You may not anticipate it, but you may have to walk some distance between offices or plant sites during your interview. Be comfortable, but stylishly conservative. If you like wearing heels, do so—but not so high that they look like evening shoes. If you select flats, make sure that they are appropriate to your outfit and that they don't look too casual.

A solid color leather pump is best. Make sure that your shoes are well polished and not scuffed.

Jewelry

Be conservative in your jewelry. A simple necklace or strand of pearls is always appropriate. Too many neck chains or bracelets do not convey a serious appearance. Earrings should be conservative, not too large nor too many. Keep rings simple and not distracting. Big, chunky jewelry, fun fakes, or jewelry from religious, fraternal, or social organizations are not appropriate.

Makeup

Makeup should be kept to a minimum. Too much eye shadow is not appropriate for the office. Simple eye makeup, powder, a bit of rouge, and lipstick will give a fresh appearance that is pleasant. If you don't know how to do your own makeup, by all means invest in a one-hour lesson from a local makeup artist or cosmetic company. Many cosmetic companies will give you a free makeup lesson if you purchase a certain amount of their products.

Handbags and Briefcases

Try not to carry both a handbag and a briefcase—the combination is too cumbersome when you have to shake hands and too much to fuss with as you enter, sit, stand, and exit. You should carry a briefcase if you are applying for any type of executive position. Try to find a leather one fitted so that you don't also have to carry a handbag. Or, if you still want to carry a handbag, choose one that fits inside your briefcase, so that you don't have to manage two items during your interview. If the briefcase has initials on it, make sure that they are yours.

Pen and Pencil

It is awkward for a woman to carry a pen and pencil in her breast pocket, so we suggest that you carry them in your briefcase. Make sure that they are easily accessible and that you don't have to fumble through a lot of rubble to find them.

6 · BE JOB SPECIFIC

You now have gathered vital information about the company you are interviewing, you understand the purpose of the interviewer's questions, and you have packaged yourself for success. The last bit of work you have to do is to gear yourself to *this* interview for *this* job. We call it being job specific.

No Two Interviews Are Identical

You must adjust your responses, your language, and often your resume for each job. As you research each company, you will begin to understand its strengths and weaknesses. You must match your strengths with the company's strengths—and, in a different way, with the company's weaknesses.

For example, if you are a creative person, skilled in product conception and execution, but not well versed in merchandising, you might be a perfect match for a company whose strength is in merchandising but which lacks the creative personnel to develop new products. You might also be a good match for a company whose merchandising is weaker because it doesn't have the right products to offer.

Planning Your Strategy

Above all, take the time to think and plan ahead. Look carefully at the situation, and think how you can position yourself as an interviewee. When you are sitting across from the interviewer is not the time to formulate your strategy.

Know the Job Specs

You should always try to learn the job specifications prior to the interview. You can then direct your conversation toward those specs, emphasizing your abilities as they directly relate to the details of the company you have learned through your research. (See Chapter 2.) However, if you have not been able to learn much about the job specs, we suggest that early in the interview you ask the interviewer to describe them for you. Then, after you have been told, you can say something like, "That's very interesting. I think I fit those requirements very well." And you will have opened a natural path for further discussion. If, on the other hand, it turns out that one of the requirements for the job is a willingness to travel 300 days per year, you had better know that at the beginning.

Know the Language

Make sure that you are fluent with the jargon of the business to which you are applying. Each business has its own language, terms, or ways of using words that are unique. Make sure that you can converse with the interviewer on his/her own terms. And, if the interviewer doesn't use any of the jargon you have learned, you can slip it into your conversation.

PART III
THE INTERVIEW

PART III

7 · INTERVIEW MECHANICS: WHERE, WHEN, WITH WHOM, AND WHY

In this Part you will learn how to handle the interview itself. We begin with interview mechanics: the who, when and where of interviewing.

Keep a Record

You will probably have several interviews during your job search. In order to remember everything about each interview, you should have a system to help you recall details. We suggest using a file or loose-leaf notebook entitled "Interviews." You should have at least three pages for each interview. They should be entitled:

Interview Mechanics
Company Information
Interview Recap

Forms for these pages appear in Appendixes A, B, and C. Sample Interview Mechanics and Company Information pages appear later in this chapter. We suggest either photocopying these pages, as required for each interview, or adapting the form to your own needs.

Finding the Information

How do you find out all the information you need for each interview? Simple: You ask the details of the interview when the meeting is being set up. If this is done by telephone, as is most likely, don't hesitate to ask detailed questions. The important thing is to be well prepared and never to go to an interview with, for example, the wrong pronounciation of the interviewer's name.

Of course, it is easier to ask these questions of a secretary or assistant rather than of the person with whom you will be meeting. But in either case, don't fail to get all of the details before you hang up.

You must have precise information regarding the following:

When and Where: You must know the exact date, time and place of the interview. Once you have been given the date and time, take the time to repeat it back to the person setting up the interview so that you are sure you have made no mistakes. Speak slowly and clearly.

The location, obviously, is crucial. Many people who are familiar with a downtown area tend to use building names, rather than street addresses. Even if you are sure that you know where the Fidelity Building is, ask for the street address, just to be sure. Also be sure to get the floor number.

Ask how long it will take you to get to the interview site from your home. Always get specific directions and mileage if possible. If the interview is in a place unfamiliar to you, make a trial run prior to the interview to familiarize yourself with the location.

If you are taking public transportation, ask for details regarding busses or trains, and confirm the information with the transportation authority or in some other adequate way prior to the interview.

With Whom: Make sure that you get the interviewer's title and name correctly, including the spelling. If the name is unusual, make sure that you have the pronounciation right. Don't be embarrassed to ask. This should not be awkward. You might say something like, "That's an unusual name. Would you mind saying it once again, so that I can be sure I have the correct pronounciation?" If you are speaking to the interviewer, your attention to detail will be impressive. If you are talking to an assistant, your uncertainty over the interviewer's name will no doubt be something he/she is familiar with.

So that you don't forget, make sure that you note the pronounciation of your interviewer's name phonetically. We believe in making notes. No matter how much attention you pay to details at the time, they have a way of flying out of your head when you need them a week later.

Form of Address: The correct form of address is very easy with a man. Call him Mister. With a woman, it's not so simple. If you are setting up the appointment with her assistant, you can easily ask the assistant if the interviewer prefers Ms., Miss, or Mrs.

If you are setting up the appointment with the interviewer, it is quite polite to ask, "Is that Ms., Miss, or Mrs.?" Once she has expressed a preference, make sure you use it, and not something else.

First Names: It is always safest to address the interviewer by his/her surname, unless the interviewer specifically asks you to use his/her first name.

Why?: Know the position you are interviewing for. If you don't ask for a clear description of the position, you may waste your time interviewing for a job that doesn't interest you, or for which you are overqualified or underqualified.

Sample Interview Mechanics and Company Information Pages

Below we have provided sample Interview Mechanics and Company Information pages. Note that all the details of the interview are covered. Complete pages similar to these for each interview.

INTERVIEW MECHANICS—B. G. BIGELOW, INC.

Date: November 4, 1988

Interviewer: Ms. Rosemary Budenstein (prefers Ms.)—pronounced as if spelled "Bewdensteen"—emphasis is on the first syllable: *Bew*-den-steen.

Title: Vice President of Development

Time: 10:00 A.M.

Place: 1500 Rainbow Road, North Building, Room 4105. Rainbow Road is off U. S. 6, 1.5 miles north of the junction of Haverford Avenue and Route 6. There's a gas station on the left just before the entrance to the Bigelow plant, which is on the right. Turn right into the driveway leading to the office complex. The North Building is the second building on the left. I can park in the first lot on the right. Tell the guard I am meeting Ms. Budenstein.

Time: Allow 45 minutes to get there. Drive should take 25 minutes—but be careful of traffic—so allow 45 minutes including parking.

COMPANY INFORMATION—B. G. BIGELOW, INC.

B. G. Bigelow is a toy manufacturer, one of the biggest in the country. Mr. Bigelow, age 82, still comes to work every day and calls himself a "toy-coon." The company prides itself on creating the Christmas sensation toy each year. However, they haven't had a big success since they did the "Tiger Lily" doll in 1982. They hired Ms. Budenstein two years ago away from the Federal Toy Company. She is supposed to be very creative, but did not produce a Christmas hit last year. The newspapers say that the company may be fading from its prominent position in the toy business because it hasn't had a Christmas hit in so many years. Ms. Budenstein has a great reputation—lots of articles about her in magazines. She was trained as an artist, and always sketches new toys herself.

Rainbow Road is the main plant. They also make some toys in Hong Kong, but prefer to maintain a "Made in America" image. They stress the "Made in U.S.A." label, and in the early 1950s became famous for their "Uncle Sam" collection. Strong patriotic spirit.

They manufacture many toys with steady sales. Specialize in cuddly, stuffed bears and doggies. Strong emphasis on the safety of their toys. Heavy consumer testing. Very child conscious.

Lots of competition. Federal is biggest. Then Allendale Toys, also located on Rainbow Road. Great rivalry.

Potential for business is enormous. Especially Christmas. They need creative thinkers with new and exciting ideas (but with attention to child safety).

The Night Before

The night before the interview, organize yourself for the next day. Don't rush around just before the interview trying to put everything together. Do it well in advance, before you are nervous and excited.

Choose your clothes in advance, right down to hose and jewelry. Don't leave anything to chance on the day of the interview. If you don't have a clean shirt, it's better to find out the night before when you still have time to wash an item or to run out to a store early the next morning. Lay out an umbrella if rain is predicted. You don't want to arrive at the interview looking wet and bedraggled.

Organize your briefcase. Make sure that you take a working pen and pencil and a pad of paper for taking notes. Include several copies of your latest resume, even though the interviewer may already have a copy. Take several copies of your typed list of references (see Chapter 17). You never know by how many people you may be interviewed, and you want to be prepared.

Take your Interview Mechanics page and Company Information page so that you can review details about the company if you have to wait. Don't take along all your research pages—that could make you appear disorganized. Take your blank Interview Recap page so that you can fill it out on the way home.

Remember Murphy

Keeping Murphy's Law in mind ("anything that can go wrong will go wrong"), set your alarm clock so that you have plenty of time the next morning. It's better to give yourself extra time than to rush and be agitated before the interview actually starts.

Try to get a good night's sleep. Go to bed early. But before you retire, read over your pages on the next day's interview. Try to memorize the pronunciation of the interviewer's name and any other names you may have discovered in your research. Re-read your research about the company. Stay calm.

The Morning of the Interview

The main rule for interview day is to allow plenty of time. This is especially true if you are taking public transportation. Make sure that you have all the bus and train schedules, and allow time for delays.

Be 15 Minutes Early

Plan to arrive at the interview 15 minutes early. This will allow you to "get acquainted" with the office and to begin to feel more at ease. You might use the time to visit the rest room for one last check in the mirror or to review your notes.

What If You're Late?

Try your best not to be late—but if it is unavoidable, immediately telephone the interviewer. Tell the interviewer or his/her assistant exactly what the problem is (a flat tire, a traffic jam, a delayed train) and give your estimate of the time you will actually arrive. Allow plenty of time, so that there will be no danger of failing this second deadline as well.

Be sure to apologize for your lateness and to point out that it was caused by a problem that you could not possibly have predicted. Express your concern that the delay has caused inconvenience. If necessary, ask if the interview should be rescheduled at a more convenient time for the interviewer.

When you do arrive, again apologize for being late. Be sure to say something like, "I'm always very punctual, and it disturbs me to have inconvenienced you when I know how busy you must be."

But don't let yourself be depressed or upset by being late. Show that you can handle the problem smoothly. Cheer up! If you are lucky, the interviewer may have needed the extra time for something else.

8 · TYPES OF INTERVIEWS

There are several major types of interviews. We will briefly cover each type to give you tips on how to handle them effectively. However, remember that the different types are only variations on the basic one-on-one interview. Your technique may vary slightly with each type, but your general battle plan remains the same.

The Informational Interview

Recent graduates and adults reentering the job market often have only a vague idea of the educational or experience requirements for a particular position. One way of gaining needed insight into a particular career is the informational interview.

This is not a job interview. Rather it is an opportunity to gain knowledge about a particular job or profession by asking questions of an expert in the area. In this type of interview, the interviewee is really the interviewer, asking questions of the job holder for the purpose of obtaining information about positions and qualifications. Never be argumentative, arrogant, or impolite during an informational interview. Remember that this person is doing you a favor by seeing you and that you owe him/her respect.

Always keep your questions brief. The length of the interview should usually be no longer than 15 minutes, unless the other person urges you to stay longer. This is a time to listen, not to talk.

We warn you that the informational interview should never be used as a ruse to get a job interview. Be very careful during an informational interview not to start asking for a job. Your purpose is to obtain information, not to sneak in by the back door. If you think that you want a job with the company and that you have the necessary qualifications, you can, in your thank-you note following the interview (see Chapter 16), state that you would like to work for the company and enclose a resume.

The informational interview is also a useful occasion to observe the type of person who might interview you if you were a job applicant. It can serve as a dress rehearsal with the roles reversed.

The Screening Interview

A screening interview is a shortcut to rejection. In it, the interviewer takes only a brief look at your basic qualifications in order to find possible reasons to reject you. The purpose is to screen you out before you move up to a more detailed level of interviewing by determining that you lack certain basic qualifications for the job or by finding, for example, inconsistencies or lies on your resume. Very often, an employment agency or search firm does the screening for a company.

If you pass the screening interview, you will then have the opportunity to move on to a real job interview. The screening interview is intended to determine if you have the basic qualifications for the job. The real job interview determines whether you are the *right person* for the job.

Nondirected and Directed Interviews

The *nondirected* interview is the most typical interview format. It means that the interviewer is not following a specific script when asking you questions, but is exploring to find the most productive paths of questioning and/or discussion as he/she goes along. If a specific script is followed, it is called a *directed* interview. Each of the following types of interviews can be either directed or nondirected.

The Stress Interview

The stress interview is less common now than formerly, but it still exists in some industries. Its purpose is to see if you can keep from getting thrown off or upset under pressure. Your response is to try to remain calm, poised, and in control.

In a stress interview, the interviewer is openly hostile, negative or critical. This type of interview—which, not surprisingly, was developed by the Germans in World War II —is used to see how you handle yourself in difficult situations.

Silence is often used in a stress interview as a technique to make you nervous. Don't feel a need to speak all the time, and once you have answered a question adequately, don't feel the need to reply further or to volunteer additional information. Simply answer the question directly and then be quiet. Your silence is perfectly acceptable if no question has been asked. Try not to look pained during silence. The ability to maintain a pleasant expression on your face in spite of stress is a point earned in your favor.

The Board Interview

There are two types of multiperson interviews: the board interview, where many interviewers are present against one interviewee, and the group interview, where many interviewees are present against one or more interviewers.

Either situation is somewhat more difficult to handle than the one-on-one interview. We will first address the easier of the two, the board interview.

In this type of interview, you are facing more than one interviewer. Each has his/her agenda regarding you, and each will have questions for you. If possible, remember each interviewer's name and use the name when responding to questions directed by that person.

The board interview is actually a form of stress interview, and you must not become flustered by the number of interviewers. When answering questions, address each interviewer as if he/she were the only other person in the room. Direct your gaze first at the questioner, and then, during your answer, include all the others in the room in your gaze.

Never get flustered if many questions are thrown at you at once. If everyone is speaking (or even shouting) at you at once, remain calm and wait for the commotion to die down. Then say that you will be happy to answer all of the questions, but that you would like to do it one question at a time. Next, select one person and address his/her question. After you have finished that answer, try to keep charge by then saying something like, "Mr. Jones, I believe you also had a question?" And so on.

One objective of this type of interview is to see how you handle yourself in a large stressful environment. Your ability to control the situation, while remaining polite and respectful, will be favorably noted and remembered.

The Group Interview

The other type of multiple interview is the group interview, where many interviewees are grouped together for questioning by one or more interviewers.

In this type of interview, your objective is to shine above the crowd. There is no simple rule for accomplishing this; you must be sensitive to the particular situation and to the apparent goals of the interviewer. Many people recommend either the "first to speak" or "last to speak" technique, on the theory that the person who answers first or last is most memorable. While we tend to agree that the last to speak is generally remembered, we recommend the "contemplative, thoughtful" approach.

Be thoughtful and consistent. Try to listen to the others in the room. Don't be overly aggressive or forceful; speak only when you have something to say or a good point to make. Always think before you speak. This type of group interview is not a television game show; you don't have to be the first to hit the button every time. A thoughtful answer is always best. You may wish to wait until most of the others have spoken so that you can compare and contrast their answers, adding your own interpretation.

The most important thing to remember is that no matter when you speak, it is what you say that is important. So think. And, in a situation like this, it is essential to speak in a well-modulated voice that does not strain, squeak, or screech.

9 · HONESTY AND MODESTY

Many people find it difficult to strike a balance between excessive self-promotion and excessive modesty. In an interview situation, you are both the salesperson and the product. While you may have been taught that it is bad taste to brag or "toot your own horn," you must also realize that you will never sell yourself convincingly unless you can communicate your virtues clearly and positively.

Tell the Truth

Communicating your virtues doesn't mean that you should twist the truth to hide your faults. The first rule of interviewing is to tell the truth. Honesty is the only policy—for many reasons, not the least of which is that you never know how much the interviewer knows about you already.

It is especially important to tell the truth regarding education or prior work experience. These things can be, and usually are, checked. If you are caught in a lie, you will not be hired.

Be Yourself

Don't try to be someone you're not. Don't "put on airs" or affectations. The interviewer is probably experienced enough so that he/she will not be fooled. Also, remember that this is a person with whom you may work for many years; you want to be accepted for what you are, not for what you aren't.

Be Positive

Be positive about your past. Even if your last employer was rude, obnoxious, and unethical—be positive. Never criticize or disparage a previous employer, since such criticism will usually backfire and put you in a poor light. All the interviewer will hear is that if you speak badly of your prior employer, you will probably speak badly of this company when you leave. On this as on other matters, always try to stress positive points in your discussion.

Never be Self-Deprecating

There is a difference between being honest and being self-deprecating. Don't apologize for weaknesses—cast them in a positive light. If you must apologize, you can't expect to be hired. After all, if *you* think your weaknesses are serious enough to interfere with your qualifications for the job, think otherwise about interviewing with this company.

This doesn't mean that you should *hide* your weaknesses. On the contrary, we believe that it is always best to take the initiative in bringing up your weaknesses and having answers prepared to explain or offset them, rather than waiting to be caught.

Accentuate the Positive

Don't be shy. If you are good at something, say so. If you don't communicate your worth, you will never get a job. Stress your good points. For example, you might point out that you are very healthy and have never missed work. Or, if you have never worked, you can stress the things you have done—such as courses you have taken and volunteer work.

Try to change weakness-requesting questions into positives. For example, if you are asked how you react to crises, you can say, "I don't enjoy crisis situations, but I am good at handling stress. Then, when the crisis is over, I am good at finding ways to avoid that type of crisis again."

Always emphasize your experience and, if it is not directly on target for the job you are seeking, look for ways to translate it into other areas of employment. For example, "I am excellent at working with people," or "I am very organized and efficient and I can learn new procedures quickly."

10 · TEN MOST COMMONLY ASKED QUESTIONS

Later in this chapter, we will introduce you to the most commonly asked interview questions. But we will begin with some general points about how questions should be answered. First of all, we would like to impress on you Rule Number 1: THINK before answering any question.

Pay attention also to Rule Number 2: BE PREPARED. Do your homework on the company. (See Chapter 2.) Then spend some time thinking about the questions you would ask yourself, if you were the interviewer. Then develop answers to those questions. (See Chapters 1 and 9.)

Remember the Purpose

All the questions an interviewer will ask of you can be summed up in one big question: Why should my company hire you and not someone else? Never forget that this is the interviewer's basic question, and direct all your responses toward answering that question successfully.

Don't Sound Memorized

While we urge you to prepare your answers carefully and thoroughly, we must caution you against sounding like a parrot when you repeat them to the interviewer. Talk conversationally, and vary your words and sentences in a way that seems natural to you.

A 50/50 Exchange

An interview should be an exchange of ideas and not a monologue. Try not to talk longer than two minutes at a time. Actually, two minutes is a long time, so we suggest that you try timing yourself while talking to understand how two minutes feels. Of course, if a question is complicated and you need a longer time to answer, take whatever time is necessary. Never be curt, but don't launch into a long monologue without good reason.

Be Interesting and Enthusiastic

Try to be interesting and not boring. Avoid phrasing your answers in a purely chronological order, because a chronology of your achievements is already in your resume. The purpose of the interview is to gain further insight into you as a person, and you should take care to emphasize what you consider interesting and important, supplementing your resume and, wherever possible, stressing strong points that may not be apparent from the resume. Show interest in and enthusiasm for this company, this job, and work in general.

Answer the Question

Try not to be like those politicians who, when asked a question, answer the question they wanted to be asked, not the question that actually was asked. An irrelevant answer suggests you may have something to hide. If, for some reason, you don't understand the question, don't hesitate politely to ask the interviewer for clarification.

Think About the Question

Many interviewers will not ask directly the question or questions they really consider most critical. Questions will be politely phrased or couched in terms that may obscure the interviewer's real meaning. Take time to consider what the interviewer is really trying to learn. The main reason for Rule Number 1—THINK before answering—is so you have time to decide on the best answer.

The Big Ten

Now for the ten most commonly asked interview questions. Make sure that you are confident of your ability to answer each of these before you even think of going to your first interview:

1. *Tell Me About Yourself.*

With this question, the interviewer opens the door for you to sell yourself or hang yourself. It is an open question that allows you great latitude in response. Be positive and to the point, emphasizing your strengths. For example, you could begin with "I am a hard worker," "I am very conscientious," or "At all my jobs, I never left until the job was done, even if it meant coming in on a Saturday." A brief elaboration following this opening declaration will get the interview off to a positive start.

Be careful of this question, however, since the wrong response can turn the interview sour. Don't voluntarily open a Pandora's box of problems. If you feel it necessary to mention negatives, do so only after laying a strong foundation of positives, and do so in a way where the weaknesses are explained or offset. Avoid any undiluted negatives.

2. *Why Are You Interested in This Position?*

This is a question that requires a great deal of thought. As it is a classic interview question, you must prepare for it carefully.

Think about your specific strengths and analyze them against the job requirements. Consider your weaknesses and think how to turn them into strengths for this specific job.

Then think about your goals and how this job fits into your long-term and short-term goals. If, for example, you want to be the head of personnel for a large company in ten years, and this job is an entry level one in the personnel department, explain how this position will put you on your career goal track.

Consider what you are looking for in a position and how this job fits your goals. Then indicate those items in your background, education, personality, and ability that make you perfect for this job. Try to be specific.

3. *Why Are You Interested in This Company?*

Here is where your research pays off. Try to be specific in your knowledge, but don't show off. Concentrate on the areas that are relevant to you, and answer this question so that the interviewer understands that you have done your homework and have considered other alternatives.

4. *Why Did You Leave Your Last Position?*

This is a question designed to find out if you are difficult to work with. Be careful not to disparage previous employers and don't cite personality conflicts as a reason for having left a previous job. You can always find a related, more palatable reason, such as the absence of promotion opportunities. Try to couch your response in a way that makes a positive out of your previous situation, even if you were fired from a job you hated by a person you loathed. For example, you could say that you had great enthusiasm for the job at the beginning, but found yourself stagnating in it because you weren't given further responsibilities and greater challenges. Emphasize that you enjoy being challenged creatively, that you enjoy working with others, and that you hope to use all your creativity in your next position.

5. *What Are Your Strengths and Weaknesses?*

Again, be positive and enthusiastic about your strengths and cast your weaknesses to their best advantage. Try to tailor your answer to suit the job. For example, if you are very creative, but not a good writer, you might say, "I am very creative and enjoy working with people. My interpersonal skills are excellent, and I have always been well-liked by my co-workers. I especially enjoy an environment where I can work and think with others, pooling our ideas to make a better product. I think that the 'open' environment of this company, about which I've heard, would give me the kind of situation in which I work best."

If you are then asked about your writing skills, you could inquire how much writing would be required for the position. If the answer is more writing than you feel comfortable with, you might say, "My verbal skills definitely are superior to my writing skills, but I did well in school in English, and I'm anxious to improve my written communications. I would consider that part of the job a challenge, and I enjoy conquering challenges."

6. *Where Do You Hope to Be in Five Years?*

This can be a trick question. The interviewer may actually be asking you, "How long do you anticipate working for this company, if you are hired?"

Answer honestly, but try to include the company in your response. Show that you have hopes and dreams and that you do not plan to stay at your current level of competence forever. Show that you have ambition.

You might answer, "My objective has been to find one company where I can grow and reach my maximum potential over the long term. I would like to make this kind of career with Company X, because I see it as a fast-growing, upwardly moving company that would offer great opportunities for me. I would expect to work hard and productively, and I would hope that in five years I would have advanced far enough to feel optimistic about my long-run future with the company."

7. *How Have Your Prior Jobs Prepared You for This Position?*

This is an opportunity not only to speak about prior job experience but also, briefly, to add anecdotal life experiences that may be applicable. For example, if the job requires organizational skills, and you have demonstrated such skills when you ran charity auctions in college, this is the time to say so.

Again, we caution you to be positive about prior work experiences. If you think that your previous job didn't fully use your organizational skills, for example, and that is one reason why you left, you might say, "While I enjoyed my previous job with Company Y, and enjoyed the interplay with my co-workers, I saw a lot of disorganization and duplication that I wasn't given the opportunity to change. I think that the experience taught me a lot that would help me streamline and organize operations here, if that should be necessary."

8. *Where Else Are You Applying for a Job?*

Be honest. If this is the only place you are applying, and you are still working at another job, phrase your response in a way flattering to the company. You might say, "Since I'm still with Company Z, and I respect the people I work with, I want to be discreet about my job search. I've tried to research other opportunities carefully and decided to target positions where there would be a really close fit between my abilities and the company. I very much liked what I read and heard about this company, and I decided to limit myself initially to this interview."

If you have many interviews set up, you could say, "I'm very anxious to explore many avenues of opportunity, and at this point I have interviews set up with Companies A, B, C, and D. I will tell you frankly, though, that I am most interested in this position because . . ." (then list reasons culled from your research, the job description, and your abilities).

9. *What Can You Do for Us That Someone Else Can't Do?*

Try to avoid the hard sell here. Of course, this is the time to be as positive about yourself as possible, but you do have to temper your selling with a sense of proportion. Try to be specific about your skills. State how you will fit in and the contributions you could make. Stress your own skills and don't disparage the possible skills of other hypothetical candidates. Combine your research on the company with your knowledge of your own abilities to give a sparkling answer.

10. *What Are Your Outside Interests?*

This is a time for you to shine as an individual. Make ·sure that you have something interesting and special to say. For example, if you love to cook, you might say, "I really enjoy cooking and love to read cookbooks and try new recipes. It's a nice way to use extra energy." If you help with the Boy Scouts, Girl Scouts, or the Police Athletic League, indicate how much you enjoy working with young people. If your hobbies are athletic, speak of the excitement and challenge of skiing or tennis.

A Final Question

Many interviewers will also ask, "What can I tell you about this company?" You should be prepared with at least two intelligent questions about the company or the job description. These questions should *not* be about salary, vacation, sick days or paid holidays. (See Chapter 12.) You want to emphasize what you will do for the company, not what the company will do for you.

Use your research to formulate areas of inquiry that show your keen interest in the company and its future. Don't be challenging, and don't ask directly about the company's possible flaws, but be intelligently, politely, and knowledgeably interested.

For example, you might use this opportunity to ask about the job description, job potential, and responsibilities. Other questions include: Does the job include travel? How often? Where? Whom would I report to? What happened to the person who had this job before? What is the potential for advancement within the company? Does the company believe in promoting from within? Try to ask questions that suggest your own intention to do serious, creative work and to grow with the company.

11 · TEN ABSOLUTE DON'TS

1. *Don't Be Late.*

Always try to be at least 15 minutes early for an interview. The extra time will allow you to become acquainted with the facility and use the rest room to freshen up. You can also use the time for relaxing your voice and calming your nerves. (See Chapter 4.)

2. *Don't Bring a Friend.*

The best advice is to arrive early and alone. Even if the person accompanying you waits in the reception room and doesn't (heaven forbid!) enter the interview room with you, the fact that you had to bring someone for support shows a lack of self-reliance and confidence that will not be judged favorably.

3. *Don't Chew Gum or Smoke.*

Chewing gum is absolutely inappropriate under any circumstances, unless perhaps you are applying for a position as taster in a chewing gum factory.

Never light a cigarette unless the interviewer specifically asks you to join him/her in a smoke. And even then, think twice before revealing your habit. As more and more states pass legislation regulating smoking in the workplace, the habit is becoming less acceptable. Showing your dependence on nicotine at an interview could work against you.

4. *Don't Forget or Abuse the Interviewer's Name.*

Always address the interviewer(s) by name and never mispronounce the name(s). If the interviewer has a difficult name, comment on how unusual it is, and then ask to have it repeated for you. This type of attention to a detail important to the interviewer is certain to please.

5. *Don't Slouch.*

Always remain standing until the interviewer offers you a chair, and once seated, maintain good posture. Don't sit so erect that you appear uncomfortable, but don't slouch, either. Poor posture conveys a subconscious feeling of sloppiness.

6. *Don't Be Negative.*

Maintain a positive and pleasant attitude during the interview. Remember that this is someone with whom you hope to work. Make sure that he/she feels that you are someone pleasant to work with.

7. *Don't Use Slang.*

Proper use of grammar and good verbal expression are keys to success. Idle chatter and overuse of slang and clichés are a road to failure. But by all means, incorporate terms of the trade into your speech, because this shows familiarity with the job and its requirements.

8. *Don't Use Gimmicks.*

Try to be pleasantly distinctive in your demeanor, style, and attitude. Try to show your individuality in your understanding of the job and the company and in your background. If you do your homework and THINK, you will never have to resort to gimmickry, which can easily backfire.

9. *Don't Be Overbearing, Loud, or Smug.*

While you want to be special, you don't want to be obnoxious. Try to strike a balance that results in a pleasantly positive, competently enthusiastic image.

10. *Don't Be A Slob.*

One of the most trying interviews is the one that occurs over a meal. This is a "do or die" situation. Be careful of what you order. Try to order something the same as or similar to what others with you are ordering. Avoid anything drippy or messy. Avoid dishes, such as lobster in the shell, which require effort to eat and will distract you from the conversation. Eat slowly. Pace yourself to the others dining with you.

It's best not to order a drink, no matter how trying the day has been and how much you really want one. Order Perrier, mineral water, or juice. However, if all the others dining with you order drinks, it may be awkward not to do the same. In this case, since you want to keep your wits about you and not to loosen up too much, order a drink that is not too strong, such as white wine, and don't hesitate to leave part of it.

12 · SALARY AND FRINGE BENEFITS

Conventional interview wisdom cautions that you should never bring up salary yourself. We agree that it is best to let the company make the decision to hire you and then negotiate salary after you are sure that you are wanted.

Know How Much Money You Need

Be clear in your own head regarding the difference between the amount of money you *need* and what you *may want*. We suggest that you review your budget so that you are clear as to how much you actually need. Occasionally, you may be offered a job which is attractive and promising for the future, but which pays poorly for the present. Your budget may then become the determining factor.

Know Your Bottom Price

So know the amount of money you will settle for if the job is right. Be clear about what you might be willing to bargain away and what you can't live without. For example, are you willing to take a cut in salary in exchange for another week's vacation? Or perhaps you are already covered on your spouse's medical plan and would prefer to earn extra salary in lieu of medical coverage.

The Plus 20 Percent Principle

Generally, of course, a more attractive job is likely to involve higher pay. Salary for a new job is usually based on what you currently earn plus about 20 percent. Sometimes the increase goes to as much as 30 percent, but this depends on the job market and the economy of the industry. Don't lie! Your current salary is too easily checked to risk the job because of a lie. Moreover, some employers will ask for a copy of your Form W-2, the annual form which reports your salary to the IRS. This request is not objectionable, but we strongly advise against providing tax returns to a prospective employer, except in special situations where this type of disclosure is required.

Doing Advance Research

Try to learn the salary range for a position before you apply. That way, if the salary is too low, you can save everyone time and effort.

Determining the salary range may require a little effort. Of course, you can ask directly, but many employers are reluctant to divulge the answer, feeling that they may be able to hire you at a bargain rate if the salary is a mystery to you.

You can try to determine what the person above you and the person below you earn. If your job is in the middle, you now have the salary range. Include salary in your library research. If the company is public, salaries of the higher officers will be disclosed in the company's proxy statement. If you know people in the business, ask what others in similar positions earn.

Search firms can be very helpful in advising on salary. (See Chapter 18.)

Fringe Benefits

As with salary, it is best not to bring up fringe benefits such as vacations, paid holidays, sick leave, insurance, medical coverage, etc., until you are sure that the employer wants to hire you.

Fringe benefits can have a high dollar value when you consider that if they weren't provided, you would have to pay for them yourself. So take the benefits into consideration when you consider the salary offered. A lower salary with very high fringe benefits may actually be worth more in real dollars than a fringeless, higher-salaried position.

Look to the Future

It is quite appropriate, during a discussion of salary, to talk about the possibility of future promotions and salary reviews. The interviewer should regard your interest in the future as healthy. You might even wish to say something like the following: "If I perform in this job as well as I tell you I am going to, how much progress in compensation could I expect after three years?"

A Hint for the Future

After you are hired, keep a chronicle of your job accomplishments so that you will have a diary of facts to rely on at salary review time. Don't trust either your memory or your bosses. Be specific, be prepared, and you will have a good chance of success.

13 · DISCRIMINATION AND ILLEGAL QUESTIONS

In general, a job applicant may not be asked any questions regarding race, sex, color, religion, national origin, or age. This right to be free from preemployment discrimination arises from Title VII of the Civil Rights Act of 1964 in combination with Executive Order 11246. It is enforced federally by the Equal Employment Opportunity Commission (EEOC). Many states also have laws prohibiting discriminatory employment practices. The agencies enforcing state laws are usually called Fair or Equal Employment Commissions or Human Relations Commissions.

What Is Discriminatory?

Unfortunately, the laws regarding discrimination in preemployment interviews are rather vague. Basically, a question is discriminatory if it asks a job applicant about his/her race, sex, religion, national origin, or age unless one of two circumstances exist: (a) there is a specific, valid reason, known as a bona fide occupational qualification (BFOQ), for the question, or (b) a gender-oriented question is asked of both male and female applicants.

For example, it is not discriminatory for an advertiser of women's lingerie to insist that lingerie models be female, because that is a reasonable BFOQ. Similarly, a woman cannot claim discrimination because a show director or producer will not cast her in the part of King Lear, a male role.

Reproductive questions, such as "When do you plan to have children?" or questions about contraception, marital status, or child care, are not permitted unless the employer asks the question of all prospective employees, male and female.

Unless an otherwise discriminatory question has a bona fide occupational qualification (BFOQ) as its basis, or a gender-oriented question is asked of both male and female applicants, the question will be viewed legally with "extreme disfavor."

"Extreme disfavor" does not mean that you would automatically win a lawsuit against an employer who asks the question. Rather, it means that the totality of the interview will be scrutinized and the intent or implication of the questioning will be reviewed. As we said, this is a vague area.

Sample Illegal Questions

"How old are you?" is one example of a question that discriminates because of age. Both younger and older applicants can suffer from having to answer this question. In addition, the courts have determined that "Have you ever been arrested?" is a discriminatory question based on race, because a disproportionate number of minority members may have been arrested but never convicted of crimes. However, an applicant may be asked if he/she has ever been *convicted* of a crime.

Your Legal Rights

If you believe that you have been discriminated against in a preemployment interview, you may file a claim with the EEOC. Your claim must be filed within 180 days. You should also file a claim with your state if it has a procedure for handling preemployment discrimination problems.

The EEOC will investigate your claim and make an attempt at conciliation. If conciliation fails and if your claim is found to be meritorious, the EEOC will issue a "right to sue" letter. Once you get this letter, an attorney can be appointed for you. However, in the interim, you must diligently try to get another job in order to mitigate your damages.

If you suspect that this whole procedure can be a big bother and may not end up very productively or lucratively, since you are obligated to mitigate your damages, you are correct. However, while suing for discrimination may not gain you much in the way of personal recovery, it will probably make the company more careful in the future.

Ignorance May Be an Excuse

If a discriminatory question has been asked, we caution all interviewees to analyze the source of the offense before jumping to conclusions. Very often an interviewer will ask a discriminatory question, not out of prejudice, but from a lack of sophistication.

If this is the case, we urge you to tread lightly. Simply pointing out that a discriminatory question has been asked may cause the interviewer sufficient embarrassment to make your point. If no offense or discrimination was intended and if the company is one where you would like to work, making an issue of the question will not get you the job. Think carefully about the question and the questioner. Reconsider if this is the type of company you want to work for. If the answer is still yes and if the answer to the question will not harm you, we suggest you answer and move to another area.

When Discrimination Is a Fact

It is one thing to answer a potentially illegal question asked out of ignorance, and another to be faced with intentional discrimination in fact.

If you find yourself in a situation where the interviewer is persistent about asking discriminatory and illegal questions, and your gentle objections fail to have an effect, you have two choices.

The first, which we have already discussed, is to file an EEOC claim. This is a difficult road to choose, with very little assurance that the results will justify the time and aggravation. Whatever your legal rights may be, in fact the filing of an EEOC claim does not often lead to a job. On the contrary, most industries are closely knit circles and filing an EEOC claim may endanger your chances of working in that industry. You may be viewed as a troublemaker and not a good candidate for employment. You may find that other interview opportunities evaporate.

Another Alternative

So, in the real world, you may prefer to take a different route in dealing with discriminatory questions. Consider the basic assumptions behind preemployment interviews. You want to work for the company, and the interviewer has the power to hire you or not. This power gives the interviewer the right to ask questions gauged to determine your suitability for the position. But the interviewer does not have the right to abuse his/her power by asking illegal questions.

You, on the other hand, have agreed to attend the interview and truthfully answer the interviewer's legitimate questions because you want the job. When the interviewer breaks his/her part of the bargain by asking an illegal question, we think, frankly, that you have a moral right to break your end of the bargain by responding with an answer that best suits your needs under the circumstances, even if the answer does not constitute the entire truth.

Since the question should never have been asked, it will be hard for anyone to fault you for giving an answer that is less than completely direct.

14 · FOR WOMEN INTERVIEWEES

This separate chapter is to help female interviewees with problems that male applicants hardly ever face.

How to Handle Compliments

If you are complimented about your looks, don't throw it back at the interviewer—unless you don't want the job or you think it's a come-on. And, even if it is the latter, you can always say no once you have the job.

How to Answer Questionable Questions

There are some questions that are irrelevant and may be asked either out of ill will or ignorance. How to respond is a challenge. Typical of these are, "Why hasn't a nice girl like you found a man to marry?" or "How does your husband like the idea of you returning to work?" or "What would you do if your husband were transferred to another state?"

We suggest that you try not to be angry or belligerent about answering questionable inquiries. Remember that the interviewer could be inexperienced and may innocently be trying to get to know you better. If the questions are suggestive of underlying prejudice but aren't actually blatant, try to formulate an answer that will put the interviewer at ease with the fact that you are well qualified for the job.

For example, the question, "Why hasn't a nice girl like you found a man to marry?" could be an awkward compliment to the effect that, "You seem so intelligent and are so attractive, I can't understand why no man has snapped you up yet." Your answer could be, "I'm sure that you meant that as a compliment, and I thank you for it. I must tell you, though, that I believe I have a lot of time to settle down, and I am more interested now in using my intellect and education to make a career in a creative environment like Company X. That is why I am applying for this job."

Regarding the question concerning how your husband feels about your returning to work, you could say, "My husband is very supportive of my career, and we have always had an understanding that I would return to work as soon as possible. He knows my abilities and is proud of my accomplishments."

In answering the question, "What would you do if your husband were transferred to another state?" you might say, "My husband and I have a 50/50 relationship, and if he were transferred, he would consider my feelings and my job before he would agree to relocate."

Try to Ignore the Offense

Again, we suggest that, if you want the job, it is best to answer the question and ignore the offense. Of course, you could gently suggest that the question is irrelevant, saying something like, "I really don't think that question is relevant to my qualifications for this job."

PART IV
FOLLOW-UP

PART IV

15 · IMMEDIATELY AFTER THE INTERVIEW

If you look at each interview as a learning process in preparation for the next interview, you will not be depressed if you fail to get an offer after your first interview, or even after the second or third.

Immediately after the interview is the time to evaluate your performance. While making notes of the questions that were asked, you should re-think your answers and decide how to answer those questions even better the next time.

Interview Recap

Immediately after the interview, note the details of the experience on your Interview Recap sheet (see Appendix C).

Fill in the interviewer's name and any relevant details regarding the office. For example, if he/she had a large sculpture of an eagle, you might note it so that you can later refresh your recollection about the interview setting. Once again, note the pronounciation of his/her name.

Note the time of the interview, its duration, and your general impression of the interviewer and the company. Were the people polite? Were they smiling? Did the place seem friendly? Did the people look happy? How easy is it to get to? Is parking or public transportation readily available and reasonable in cost?

Note any personal details you want to remember. For example, if the interviewer loves ballet and you discussed your mutual admiration for the Bolshoi, note it. Also note what you wore to the interview.

Remember that your objective in filling out the Recap is so that you can refresh your recollection if you get called back for another interview or to be given a job offer. After several interviews, you probably won't remember the details of each unless you take time to make this kind of written record. Yet knowing which was which is essential so that you don't become confused on the next round.

16 · THANK-YOU NOTES

A thank-you note has become a standard postinterview practice, and we strongly urge you to send one no later than the day following the interview. In the note you can actually ask for the job, assuming you want it. You may want to reiterate some points of your conversation, so that the interviewer remembers who you are, and you should again thank the interviewer for his/her kindness. Some individuals include in the note a brief summary of what they could do for the company and a reiteration of relevant past successes; if you can do this deftly, it may be a good idea, but it's not required.

Always Leave on a Positive Note

Sending a note thanking the interviewer(s) for spending time with you leaves everyone with a positive impression of you. Remember that the future is hard to predict, and the fact that you may not have gotten this job does not mean that you might not get a job there in the future.

So we urge you to send a thank-you note, even if you know that you did not get the job. Remember that there may be many circumstances, unrelated to you or your qualifications, that influence the hiring decision. Your failure to get the job could mean simply that your specific qualifications didn't fit the specific needs of this job, not that you aren't generally well qualified.

Multiple Notes

If you have met or been interviewed by more than one person, it helps to send a separate note to each individual. This extra bit of personalized attention always leaves a good impression.

It's a Small World

Most occupations are small worlds of their own, and people in a particular business either personally know, or know of, others in it. We know of one real estate attorney who was relocating his family from Houston to Philadelphia. He was exceptionally well qualified, with an outstanding undergraduate and law school record and two years' experience with a well-known Houston firm. He interviewed at ten Philadelphia law firms and received ten offers. He decided to accept the offer at the firm where he felt most at ease and began work in Philadelphia on July 5. On July 6, to his shock, the entire real estate department of the firm left en masse, leaving him alone in a department that formerly numbered 11. With only two years of law practice under his belt, he felt that he needed the guidance of other experienced attorneys, and so he also departed on the 6th.

He immediately contacted the other firms he had interviewed. After each interview, he had sent gracious thank-you notes to each person he met. He had also sent each firm a letter explaining his decision not to accept their offer. Because he had kept the doors open and never burned his bridges, he was able to call them, and he immediately received several new job offers. He began working with his new firm the next day.

PART V
IMPORTANT
MISCELLANY

PART V

17 · A WORD ABOUT REFERENCES

Your job-hunting equipment should include a neatly typed list of the names, titles, addresses, and telephone numbers of five to seven persons who have agreed to serve as references for you, and several copies of this list should accompany you to every interview.

Choosing References

References must be chosen with great care. Never include someone whose knowledge of you is slight, simply because his/her name sounds impressive. If you include a United States senator on your list, make sure that the senator personally knows who you are and can speak in positive terms about you.

Get Prior Approval

Always contact the reference personally before using his/her name at an interview. Make sure that the person agrees to speak or write a letter on your behalf. You should discuss the types of jobs you are applying for and the job qualifications, indicating to the reference precisely what you would like him/her to emphasize.

A Tip

If you have an interview for a job you absolutely want, you might ask one or two of your references to call the interviewer before they are called. Pick only those individuals who can speak knowledgeably and positively about you and your work. Of course, as this is an imposition on the reference, you can't do this often, but it can be powerfully impressive to an interviewer if a reference takes the time to initiate a communication on your behalf.

18 · HOW TO USE A SEARCH FIRM

A search expert, also known as a headhunter or recruiter, can be an invaluable tool in your job search. A search firm can serve as a resource to match you with the right job, help you through the interview process, walk you through salary negotiations, and evaluate your potential worth to a particular company. In addition, the credibility of a top-notch search firm almost always rubs off on its candidates.

Be Honest

It is essential that you be totally honest and up-front with any search firm you use. If you are found to have lied, or even to have withheld facts that should have been disclosed, you will ruin your chances of ever working with that firm again.

Types of Search Firms

There are two basic types of search firms: retainer-only and contingency firms. It is important to understand that both types work for the company, not for the individual. A *retainer-only* firm receives a retainer from the client company. Most executive search firms are strictly retainer-only. *Contingency* firms do not work on a retainer; instead, they are paid by the company only if they find a candidate to fill a specific position. Many search firms are combinations of both approaches.

Specialist Firms

Search firms frequently specialize in certain occupations, such as law, engineering, health care, or architecture. The more specialized the firm, the more precise the search. An experienced firm in a given field understands and knows the people and the profession. If you are in an occupation where there are specialized headhunters, you are most likely to be successful if you can use one or more of these specialist firms.

The Company Pays the Fee

Remember that, no matter if the firm is retainer-only or contingency or a combination, the company pays the fee. Never work with a search firm that makes you pay a fee. Never.

Where to Find Search Firms

Your library or your high school or college placement office should have lists of reliable recruiters in your area. Ask friends, relatives, or acquaintances who work in your occupation for the names of headhunters they know. The telephone classified book will give you a complete listing, but not much more information than names. One excellent book, *The Directory of Executive Recruiters* published by Kennedy and Kennedy, Inc., Templeton Road, Fitzwilliam, N. H. 03447, should be available at your local library.

How to Get a Headhunter to Work for You

You should try to reach as many search firms as possible. Remember that these firms are working for their client companies, not for you; your job is to convince them that you are an attractive candidate to present to their clients. However, it is not out of place for you to ask questions. Your purpose is to evaluate the credibility of the person and the firm you are talking to. Ask what types of positions the firm has filled recently. Ask what client firms and what types of specific positions they deal with. Ask what situations they have available that might suit your qualifications and use your charm and knowledge to convince the headhunter that, if given interviews, you will be a strong and capable job candidate.

Sending unsolicited resumes to search firms may not produce much in the way of response, but it is a reasonable way to begin, especially if you have no personal introductions to recruiters. In particular, we suggest sending your resume to any specialized firms in your field because they will know what is available and will be more likely eventually to find something for you.

Remember that retainer-only search firms conduct pinpointed searches for a client company. It will require some luck for your unsolicited resume to fit the positions they are currently trying to fill. We suggest that you call such firms and ask them what types of jobs they are currently filling. If they do not have anything suitable for you, but tell you to send a resume to add to their files, do so, but don't expect any quick response.

If you interview a search firm and they sound excited and positive about your prospects of getting job interviews, be sure to keep in touch with the person you met. You might send the recruiter a thank-you note, just as you would a job interviewer. (See Chapter 16.) Be careful not to become a nuisance by phoning too often. As one recruiter told us, there is a fine line between keeping in touch and harassment. Be sure to keep on the right side of that line.

Conflicts

If you contact and are working with more than one search firm, you may run into the problem of conflicts between them. Conflicts are most likely between specialists who work in the same area. A conflict could arise, for example, between two contingency firms who both submit you for the same job. In order to avoid this potential problem, we suggest that you let each search firm you are working with know that you are also registered with other firms. While this may not preclude conflicts, it at least lets everyone know that they are not your exclusive representative.

A search firm may tell you that they have a position in mind for you and ask you to wait a reasonable period of time (not more than a week to ten days) before contacting other headhunters. This is especially likely in the case of contingency firms, who tend to be more aggressive because they don't get paid unless they actually place a candidate in a job. In this situation, you should evaluate the firm and the position they offer, asking as many details as possible. Try to get a sense of how the firm evaluates your chances of actually getting hired. If their answers are satisfactory, and if the job sounds interesting, you may refrain from contacting other search firms until the time has elapsed. A retainer-only firm gets paid whether the position is filled or not.

Let the Headhunter Prepare You

In addition to getting you the interview, a good search firm will prepare you for it. You should be given annual reports of the company and other relevant material. Of course, you will still have to do work on your own, and you must prepare for the interview carefully. (See Chapters 1 and 2.) If the person you are working with at the search firm doesn't prepare you for the interview, but you are otherwise satisfied with the firm, consider changing to another person within the same office.

Ask the recruiter about the people he/she has placed at the company in the past. Remember that the recruiter has already discussed the position with the firm and no doubt knows about the person who will interview you. Let the recruiter be your guide to the interview.

Sanford L. Fox, chairman of a major executive search firm, told us that most people out of work lost their job not because of technical incompetence, but because of chemistry. He pointed out that the "culture" of a company and its history are the most important items a recruiter can prepare you about. An experienced headhunter understands the company he/she is working with and will be able to tell you about the company and the person who will interview you. This gives you the maximum opportunity to match your approach to the company and to the interviewer's chemistry.

After the interview, use the recruiter for feedback about your interview performance. Should your interview be successful, you will also find a headhunter invaluable during salary negotiations. He/she should be able to "walk you through" the salary negotiations, giving you important advice on everything from how much salary to request to the relative value and merits of various perks and fringe benefits.

APPENDIX A

INTERVIEW MECHANICS

Name of Company:
Date of Interview:
Time of Interview:
Place of Interview:
  Directions:

Name of Interviewer:
  Pronounciation:
Title of Interviewer:

Title of Job Being Offered:

Job Qualifications:

APPENDIX B

COMPANY INFORMATION

Name of Company:
Main Location:

Main Product or Service:
Subsidiary Products or Services:
Branches or Subsidiaries:
Manufacturing Locations:
Other Locations:

Company History:
   Year Founded:
   Publicly or Privately Owned:
   Annual Sales ($):
   Annual Net Earnings ($):
   If Public, Where Stock Is Traded:
   Recent Price of Stock:
   Price Range over Past 5 Years:

Competition:
Potential:

Other Comments:

APPENDIX C

INTERVIEW RECAP

Date of Interview:
Length of Interview:
  Starting time:
  Ending time:
What I Wore:
Name(s) of Interviewer(s):
  Pronounciation:
Title(s) of Interviewer(s):
General Impression of Interviewer:
  Attitude of interviewer:
  Key questions asked:
Details of Office:
Any Other Memorable Details:
General Impressions:
  Location:
    Accessibility:
    Parking:
    Public transportation:
    Cost of parking or public transportation:
    Time to get to work:
  Co-workers:
    Polite?
    Smiling?
    Pleasant environment?
  Working conditions:
  Other:

INDEX

ABOUT THE AUTHORS

PHYLLIS C. KAUFMAN, the originator of the *No Nonsense Guides*, is a Philadelphia attorney and theatrical producer. A graduate of Brandeis University, she was an editor of the law review at Temple University School of Law. She is listed in *Who's Who in American Law, Who's Who of American Women, Who's Who in Finance and Industry* and *Foremost Women of the Twentieth Century.*

ARNOLD CORRIGAN, noted financial expert, is the author of *How Your IRA Can Make You a Millionaire* and is a frequent guest on financial talk shows. A senior officer of a large New York investment advisory firm, he holds Bachelor's and Master's degrees in economics from Harvard and has written for *Barron's* and other financial publications.